Clarity: Seeking

Haikus for a Beginning

Robin M. White

BookLeaf
Publishing

India | USA | UK

Dedication

To those starting a new phase.

Preface

A new year. A new beginning.

After 30 years I retired from state government effective 01/01/2025. It is exhiliarating and scary, exciting and nerve racking, joyful and sad!

Will I have enough money to do what I want? For that matter, WHAT will I do? My daily routine was well honed over the years for me to accomplish both work and personal tasks and goals. The structure provided a safe framework for me to work, play, explore, and discover.

For the past few years I have chosen a word of the year and have embodied that word with varying success. This year, given the new journey I will be navigating, I expanded that concept and chose the following as my touchstones:

Word - Clarity
Color. - Yellow
Animal - Owl
Talisman - Third Eye
Hashtag. - #yellowglowofclarity

Mantra. - I open my intellect and my soul to the positive
yellow energy of clarity

The haikus in these pages are me stumbling to find a
foothold in my new reality. and seeking to embody
clarity as I travel this path.

Please join me on this journey.

Acknowledgements

To those who know.

1. Time

1

Quietly she peeks
in the future. What will come?
Bliss? Abyss? She waits.

2. See

2

Clarity seeping -
new day. Joy, anxiety
war. Who will light path looming?

3. Search

Adrift. Untethered
from times past. Abyss surrounds;
seeking points of light.

4. Breathe

Waiting. Unknown looms.
Spectre devouring joy,
instilling fear, angst.

5. Choose

Divergent streams flow,
calling. Quiet vibrations
light path of true north.

6. Fear

Edge of sanity.
Clarity imminent? Or
into precipice?

7. Move

Gather shards of self.
Drop sharp edges. Cut. Bleed. Heal.
Sight sharpens to truth.

8. Doubt

Monday - ill at ease.
Not back to daily normal.
What to do with hours?

9. Struggle

Reaching for the line,
fighting resistance, stubborn
in face of the next.

10. Seek

Days merge, a swirling
miasma of disquiet. The
way glimmers faintly.

11. Arrive

New truth seeping
through haze of denial. Gaze
along edge of cliff.

12. Regress

Rage shimmers; surface
ripples. Facade slips, reveals
truth lurking within.

13. Accept

Breathe. Allow moments.
Joy. Doubt. Feat. Ire. All fleeting.
Pursue clarity.

14. Pursue

Rhythms hazy, sway,
teetering on razor's edge,
chasing rhythm's voice..

15. Duel

One fighting - all in -
to live. Other in endless
woe is me vortex.

16. Grief

Leave it with the Lord.
I believe. Yet fight truth that
scorches soul. I wept.

17. Squall

Time? Just a construct?
Does reality exist?
Floating, rudderless.

18. Jangle

Waiting. Unknow looms.
Spectre devouring joy,
instilling fear, angst.

19. Flight

Beauty in the clouds.
Colors muted - soft, floating,
wisps in grey-blue sky.

20. Allow

Threads fray. Tapestry
morphs, edge's bleeding. Patterns
fight yet surrender

21. Rest

Elusive vapors,
ephemera dancing to
edge of night. Slumber.

www.ingramcontent.com/pod-product-compliance
Lightning Source LLC
LaVergne TN
LVHW021347200726

843509LV00014B/2717